How to Train

Your

Manager!

The Art of Managing UP

By

Darlene Stuart Goddard

D S Goddard

This book is dedicated to:

Donald Goddard, my husband of 40 years who helped by being my better half fulfilling those areas where he excels, allowing me to focus on my career and now this book. He is my anchor, beacon, and North Star.

Table of Contents

Introduction

Congratulations on buying this book. We have all heard the horror stories, hilarious gaffs, and plain "What were they thinking?" tales of *Epic Management Failures*. (I have a boat load of them based on my personal experience in the trenches.) But this book isn't about rehashing the classic 'bad boss' examples.

I want to look at the employee/manager relationship from a different perspective. Most managers are not "bullies" as some people believe. They are just untrained and doing the best they can with little or no ability to "get the work done through others" effectively.

We all have a manager, and that manager has someone to answer to. Even the president and CEO are in their positions at the pleasure of the company's owners, partners, stakeholders, or even financial institutions.

Statistics over the last fifty-plus years show the largest percentage of voluntary employee turnover is attributable to the person's **direct supervisor!** It hovers around 75% to 80% of all employee quits every year.

Our manager holds our future with the company in her hands.

How we interact with the person to whom we report has a direct effect on our continued employment, potential for promotion, and future income. Most importantly, however, the quality of our relationship with our manager has an enormous effect on our personal life, health, and well-being.

As employees, we all have a stake in our manager's success or failure. We even have some influence on our manager's future direction. How?

My ideas on this are here, in this book. Take what resonates with you and try it! If you are a manager, you may see yourself on both sides of this relationship coin!

Enjoy!

Darlene

PART I: What Is Managing Up?

We Are All Stakeholders in Our Manager's Success

Let's start with a definition of the word *manage*. Here are the results from Dictionary.com.

Definition:

- be in charge of (a company, establishment, or undertaking); administer; run.
- administer and regulate (resources under one's control).
- have the position of supervising (staff) at work.
- be the manager of (a sports team or a performer); maintain control or influence over—control, handle, master; cope with, deal with.
- be in charge of, run, be head of, head, direct, control, preside over, lead, govern, rule, command, superintend, supervise, oversee, administer, organize, conduct, handle, guide, be at the helm of.
- *informal*—head up

What defines a good manager who has leadership skills? People will follow her if they can answer *yes* to the three following questions:

- Do you care about me?
- Are you committed to helping me?
- Can I trust you?

Think about the best leader/manager you've ever worked for. Did she personally care that you were safe, happy, healthy, empowered, challenged, successful? Was she as committed to the project as she expected you to be? Did she just expect you to make her look good?

Relationships thrive in business, and the best leaders do the following without exception.

1. Be Fair—Do the right thing
2. Be Frank—Tell the truth
3. Be Firm—Mean what you say
4. Be Friendly—Don't be an asshole
5. Be Faithful—Do what you promise

This covers a wide range of positions, from the team leader all the way through the chain of command to the Corporate Headquarters (C-Suite). However, sometimes it will include people without a title or defined job duties who also maintain, influence, handle, cope with, deal with, and guide! In other words, people who are already exhibiting Managing Up skills!

One special note: Rather than using he or s/he, I've decided for simplicity and the editor's sanity to use the feminine pronouns when referring to managers. This is not a condemnation of female skills or letting male managers off the hook! Quite the opposite, actually. As a gender, females surpass males in managerial skills, as several management effectiveness studies have already shown! (Gallup, Inc. – 2015 State of the American Manager report. 2016 University of California, Davis study. 2016 – Peterson Institute for International Economics – Is Gender Diversity Profitable? Evidence from a Global Survey.)

Chapter 1: The #1 Way to Positively Effect Change

Our ability to improve conditions in our workplace diminishes the farther down the chain of command our position sits. But it doesn't mean we are powerless! We can make a difference in our co-workers' and customers' lives by building our influence muscle.

The payoff is that we enjoy the fruits of this exercise in so many ways at work and beyond.

It Takes a Village

You've heard the saying "A rising tide lifts all boats." How well we do our job has a direct effect on the productivity and profitability of our whole department. Our supervisor's job also depends on how well we and our team perform.

The converse is we are only able to do our jobs well with good leadership! A supervisor who is unskilled at managing (see definition in Part 1) hamstrings her team and puts up roadblocks employees must navigate around to do their best work.

It Helps to Learn the Lingo

Every workplace has its own language. Familiarizing yourself with the acronyms, terms, and word usage is part of learning your duties.

CAUTION: Newbies are often exposed to derogatory slang terms used by the team out of earshot of the managers. Before you use any office slang, be sure you have a clear understanding of the meaning of those words. Avoid derogatory slang in most cases.

Note the two terms in the preceding section: **productivity** and **profitability**. These two terms are expressed in numbers and looked at closely by the ownership. These numbers are how your department, and by extension the entire management structure, is judged.

Productivity—How many…

- widgets did we produce?
- sales did we make?
- days did we meet our goal?

Profitability—The difference between…

- income (the money coming in the door) and
- expenses (the money going out the door)

A manager's performance is also measured by other indicators, such as employee turnover, safety inspections, customer feedback, and so on. Her performance is also compared against other departments within the company and against competitor performance in these and other areas.

Did You Know Most Team Leaders and Supervisors Have Not Been Trained to Manage People?!

We all know the team leader who is the best at doing the job. They often have seniority. They are the fastest, most efficient, and know all the subtle things to do and to look out for when getting the job done right. "Of course—management picked her for team leader," you say. But do team leaders know how to manage other people to do the job? Often, their only clues are copying manager behavior they have experienced in their personal and work lives.

I once had a manager who was a ruthless, no-nonsense, "my way or the highway" boss. His management style was so different from the person he was outside of work! I could not reconcile his Jekyll/Hyde personalities until I learned his dad was a drill sergeant in the military. We realized, then, that he was imitating his father's "management" style. Once we brought that to his attention, he became more collaborative and a thoughtful supervisor.

Note: I did not learn management skills through training or any instruction, either. I had a lot of different jobs during the early years, working after school and at various full- and part-time jobs. Some of my managers then were good managers, some were poor managers, and a couple were horrible bosses.

It wasn't until I started working for Larry Aiken of Aiken Management that I got an inkling of just how amazing working for a skilled manager could be. Larry was an event promoter by the time I worked for him, but he had previously been an entertainer and radio personality known as Lonesome Larry. I think he learned his management skills through his ability to LISTEN to his audiences, to know what they liked or needed, and to help them feel validated and part of a group or tribe.

Watching Larry accomplish amazing things through managing other people was a master's-level course for me. By applying the question "What would Larry do?" I was able to grow into management and specialize in HR over the next few years.

Larry always asked his team their opinions and ideas before he made a move. He made us feel we were part of the decision-making process. He welcomed input from all of his team members and often applied those ideas into the process. No wonder he had a group of employees who would 'go to the mat' for him!

Chapter Summary/Key Takeaways

Our success is dependent upon our department's and our manager's performance as well as our own contributions.

Just because a manager exhibits a certain style does not mean it is her default personality. She may be emulating a parent's, teacher's, coach's, or previous manager's behaviors simply because it's her only reference or example of how to manage others.

Productivity and **profitability** are the measurements by which our department—and by extension, our manager and our success—is weighed.

In the next chapter, you will learn a fabulous team-building skill.

Chapter 2: Protect Colleagues from Management

I had a CEO who frequently explained to his management team that part of his job was to protect the staff from them! Yes, it is the job of anyone in the senior leadership team to make sure the subordinate management behaves according to policies, regulations, laws, and standards to get the work done. However, once the awareness of issues has come to the C-Suite level, things have gone too far for an easy and inexpensive repair. Many times, even the manager's continued employment is at risk!

We all have heard or experienced episodes of the "Bad Boss Behavior." Who usually suffers? The team members she directly supervises.

Is the Right Person in the Right Seat on the Bus?

One of the most common sources of this conflict goes to having the right skills in the wrong position on the team. By just pointing out Fred, the maintenance guy, is really good with numbers and Jane, the receptionist, is the one everyone else asks when the copier goes out, we give our manager a clue. Perhaps they could perform better in other positions where the tasks better meet their natural talents.

When you realize your manager may not be in the right seat herself, it can explain so much! Managers are made, not born, though. With the right help and support anyone can learn techniques to manage and control much of the conflict and drama being created in the department.

Knowing your manager's habits, likes, and dislikes also helps you to better coach your co-workers on how and when to approach the manager with news and ideas.

Where Is the conflict?

Conflict usually has a starting point. It could be something as simple as the boss not saying "hello" one morning! REALLY! For example, one of our team members just suddenly shut down. His production numbers tanked, he started eating lunch in his car instead of socializing with the rest of the crew, and the manager was upset and wanted to fire him after losing a time bonus she felt his lowered performance was responsible for!

When I spoke with the guy about the change in his production and demeanor, he asked, "What is the use?" He was sure he was going to be fired anyway because the manager had been mad at him for weeks. After finding out his change in behavior was the direct result of his extreme reaction to her 'snubbing' him one morning, I was able to get the two talking. Results: Employee's job—saved; manager—lesson learned; production—back on track!

Things Usually Do Not Change without Action!

Jane was always late to work. This had been going on for a long while and her co-workers, knowing of serious personal challenges she was going through, had given her grace by picking up the slack. However, everyone now knew things were on the upswing at home and Jane was moving forward personally.

The manager called one morning to tell HR a group of Jane's co-workers had come to her office asking when she was going to fire Jane for continuing to be late! It seems they were now feeling Jane was taking advantage of them.

After discussing a plan with HR, the manager pulled the time sheets, circled all the late clock-ins, and was amazed.

She had not been paying attention. Jane's co-workers were right. Jane was put on notice, and with only a few slip ups, she improved her habits and ultimately became able to take the opening shift due to her excellent attendance record.

The people who know the most about what is going on are the ones who do the work every day. Our manager has her own jobs to do, reports to send, and meetings to attend. She often gets lost in the whirlwind swirling right on her desk. By helping our manager keep in touch with the crew, we can provide a valuable conduit to help keep small problems small and solvable!

Things Usually Do Not Change Overnight!

Wouldn't it be nice to wave our magic wands and remove all the drama from our workplaces? Well, it won't happen quickly or even completely, but by being the eyes and ears for your team and your manager, small conflicts can be nipped in the bud.

One way to gauge your progress is to take stock of where you were/are at the beginning of your conscious attempts to become a successful trainer of your manager. Set a reminder to review your improvement every six months or so. Then when it seems you're moving two steps backward instead of forward, look back to the way it was before. This simple exercise will remind you although there are setbacks, you are still moving in the right direction.

Chapter Summary/Key Takeaways

Protecting your team from ill-advised management actions and decisions is every employee's job.

Making sure small problems and issues are resolved quickly ensures the problems do not travel up the chain of command.

When you help the team develop direct conversations with the manager, it improves communication all around. The more empowered the team is to give feedback and to propose ideas for improvement, the better the whole department will perform.

Limiting the drama in the workplace benefits everyone who would be exposed to it, both inside and outside the team.

In the next chapter, you will learn…

WIIFM! (What's in It for Me)—Helping your manager succeed has so many additional benefits for your own success at work and in life.

PART II: Who Benefits?

It never ceases to amaze me how small changes can make a big difference. The more we experience, the more we learn from them, both good and bad.

- Sometimes it's a lesson how *not* to do or say ____ (you fill in the blank ☺).

- Sometimes the experience sparks our creativity. This is the recipe for continuous improvement.

Chapter 3: YOU!

What are you good at *now* that was a disaster the first time you tried it? What did you learn from the experience?

Managing people is nothing more than relating to them and understanding how *they* like to engage with others and tasks.

By exercising our observation muscle and mentally asking *why*, we improve our investigative skills!

Applying and Refining Lessons from the Past

It is unpleasant and embarrassing to think back on some of the horrible mistakes we've made relating to other people. Things like:

- Making other people cry

- Destroying a friendship over ill-timed harsh words

- Repeating gossip only to find out the story was completely false

- Being manipulated by someone with their own agenda

- Not making the initial contact and never getting to know a new friend

Making these mistakes and others is all part of growing. Viewing those negative experiences as examples of what *not* to do or say is how we learn to try other ways to behave.

Improving the Present Day-by-Day

By continuing to apply lessons learned and stretching our courage muscle, we can continue to grow and evolve all of our relationships, not just the ones at work.

We do spend more of our waking hours at work, though! And by making small improvements in your own performance as well as helping others with ideas and observations, you will begin to see progress.

Recognizing even small team-wins will add sparkles to an otherwise humdrum day. And when a crew member improves, or their idea gets adopted, a small impromptu celebration is in order.

Creating a Longer Time Horizon

"Thank god it's Friday/Oh god, it's Monday" is no way to live. So many are living paycheck-to-paycheck and feel like a rat in a wheel.

If this is you, it is time to start thinking farther ahead and setting some goals. When you start to develop your influencing skills in your life, you are looking out for and working toward the future.

Walking a Mile in Others' Shoes

The more you can understand *why* a person says or does the things she does, the better you can relate to her. Growing the ability to empathize with others increases your capacity to help effect positive change in the relationship.

Changing Perspective on the Future

The future is a moving target. When we step outside our comfort zone, we learn and we grow. The increased abilities we gain in relating to and dealing with other people have an effect on our possible future opportunities! In his book

The Power of Now, Eckhart Tolle describes ways we can get out of our own mind so we can just be present in and focus on today. When we agonize over the uncertainties of the future and regrets of the past, the additional stress we place on our body and mind affects our health and well-being, too. (Readers, this book is a gift to your future self.)

Developing a Bulletproof Mindset

You have heard the saying "This too shall pass." Very few things occur in our lives we can't get over or adjust to. When nervousness, anxiety, and fear emerge about anything, it is hard to think through and respond instead of reacting. It is built into our genes.

The 'fight, flight, or freeze' effect we experience is in response to the adrenaline those emotions release automatically into our body. When we practice our observation and asking-why skills, these fear responses can be overcome.

If we use FEAR as an acronym, it can be spelled out as: False Evidence Appearing Real. I have a process to control my fear when my heart starts beating fast and I become excessively nervous or fearful. It starts with answering two questions:

1. "What if the absolutely worst thing happens?" If the worst thing is something I can plan against and/or recover from, then anything else is entirely manageable.

2. "What difference will it make a month from now?" As I contemplate both of these questions and think of the possible answers, my anxiety starts to lessen and my pulse calms down. The BEST part is when I take the time to ponder the possibilities—then all sorts of ideas and other opportunities pop into my head!

Developing Your "Unintended Consequences" Radar

Murphy's Law is a real thing. Some examples of Murphy's Law are:

- If there are two or more ways to do something, and one of those ways can result in a catastrophe, then someone will do it that way.

- It will take longer and cost more.

- You never find a lost article until you replace it.

- Left to themselves, things tend to go from bad to worse.

- Enough research will tend to support your theory.

- The opulence of the front-office decor varies inversely with the fundamental solvency of the firm.

It seems to affect people the most who have the least-effective UC Radar. While helping your supervisor and team move forward, you personally are also learning and growing. One of the benefits is learning to use the logic exercises of imagining all the ways Murphy's Law can derail the plan.

Playing devil's advocate well is a more valuable skill than you may think! Stopping to think "what if…" helps us plan for and/or defend against those potholes in the road to success we may be overlooking. One question a devil's advocate asks: "If this plan is wildly successful, will you be able to keep pace with demand?"

Believe it or not, many young companies die from extreme success. The stress on the employees with the production demand, the strain on cash flow, increasingly unhappy customers, and failure to defend against competitors jumping onto the successful company's lucrative idea are all things a strong devil's advocate could have predicted.

Practice Tip

Think back on an impulse purchase or a snap decision you've made. Grab a pen and jot it down. Next, list answers to these three questions:

1. Were there any unintended consequences you experienced as a result?

2. What other consequences could have happened but fortunately didn't occur?

3. If you had taken the time to consider the possible repercussions of your decision, what would you have done differently?

Planning for Changes

The often-quoted definition of the Chinese word for *crisis* is the combination of two characters, representing danger and opportunity. Although a good way to approach some crisis scenarios, this definition is not actually true. However, there is a great Chinese phrase translated as "opportunity accompanies crisis/challenge." This phrase *is* often used to describe a time of change in Mandarin Chinese.

Not long ago, I received an estimate on repairing my 2001 Hyundai Elantra and found it was going to cost over $1,300. OUCH! Now, it wasn't about the money as much as that I did not want to *change* my car. Did I mention I loved it?! She was my "little baby car." She was the first car I had bought new, off the showroom floor. It had taken me through many professional changes and on many long and short trips all over the place. In fact, she had provided over 234,000 miles of lovingly dependable transportation for me.

I researched to find out her resale value was only $1,200. I took her to another repair shop and decided to pay for the immediate repairs and keep her rather than *changing*. The repairs worked for only a short time before I was back in the same situation, though.

I am ashamed to say I agonized over the decision when the facts were pretty obvious. She was no longer cost-effective, dependable transportation for me.

Change was staring me hard in the face with the clock ticking. It was time to let go. I had to do something different, but what?

All of a sudden, *options* started to come to mind! I could buy a new car. I could find a much newer used car and save thousands of dollars. I could even rent a car to give me time to shop for the replacement. I could use my husband's truck for a while. I found out we had access to Uber drivers in our little town, too!

Long story short, I am now driving a much newer, slightly larger, and much more comfortable sedan with only 78,000 miles on the odometer. I saved nearly $20,000 over buying the same vehicle new. My auto insurance premium even went down significantly due to the improved safety features in this newer model! And by the way, I *love* my new(er) car!

We all have change coming into our lives. In fact, the only constant in life *is* change. The sooner we face the probability of change coming, the better we can prepare and start looking for all the opportunities and options this change is going to create.

Chapter Summary/Key Takeaways

One of the most rewarding benefits from learning to train our manager is how it develops our own resilience and ability to recover from the unexpected things thrown in our path at work and in life.

In the next chapter, we will discover how to answer your manager's WIIFM questions.

Chapter 4: Your Manager

Wouldn't it be nice to work with a superior who you respect and admire? Your supervisor would probably like to be that person! She often just doesn't know how, doesn't even know it is possible, and does not have anyone to coach her toward becoming better. Looking at what's in it for her helps us frame our discussions in ways to appeal to her self-interest.

Reducing the Drama

Are the day-to-day interactions within the team contentious? It does not have to be that way!

A strong manager with a coaching mindset solves the disruptions early and decisively.

A manager who displays the willingness to hear problems, complaints, and issues will gain the team's esteem.

A manager who invites ideas from team members and who publicly gives the credit to them will gain loyalty.

A manager who establishes expectations (not rules) and makes sure everyone knows when they are or aren't being met will have few discipline issues.

Improving Status within the Company

Does the team consistently meet and exceed the goals set by her manager and the company? Your manager cannot do it alone! The actual job of a manager is to "get the work done through others."

How well the team performs reflects directly on the capability and skill of the direct supervisor and, by extension, her manager. If there are higher costs and lower productivity, for example, they will show on the monthly reports. And all management in the chain of command reviews these numbers regularly, usually each month.

Improving the Relationship with Her Superior

As noted above, the manager's performance directly affects her manager's results and therefore performance of the larger work group. Whether you apply them consciously or not, some of the tools you utilize with your manager will probably rub off on her. The more she can improve her interaction with her boss in addition to boosting productivity within the department, the better.

Being More "In the Know"

If there is a serious issue, your manager needs to know about it before her manager does. One of the absolute worst feelings in the world is to be called into the senior manager's office only to be blindsided!

Getting a heads-up from you helps her prepare for the eventual crisis meeting. By having the opportunity to mitigate or correct the situation before she tells her boss about it, she will gain brownie points and by extension her whole team will, as well. Good managers depend on the team to be their eyes and ears. Her boss depends on her to keep informed of issues affecting the department and the company as a whole. Being able to quickly determine the facts, learn the current status of the situation, and summarize the next steps the team will take gives your team the roadmap to resolution.

Chapter Summary/Key Takeaways

Helping your manager perform at a higher level increases her status in the company and improves her relationships with other management. The biggest payoff by far is the reduced day-to-day drama within her department!

In the next chapter, we will take a look at benefits our other stakeholders in the work product will enjoy.

Chapter 5: Everyone Else at Work

So many people are affected by our department's productivity or lack thereof. I'm focusing this chapter on the people who get the results of the work, internally and externally.

Human Resources Department

I could do a whole book just on the drama creeping into and landing with a loud *whump* at Human Resources' doorstep. The best employees in HR find themselves coaching and training managers at all levels on employee relations. Much of what moves over to HR would be much better handled at the moment of friction between the participants.

Having to get senior management involved in the problem is a consequence of letting the dispute rise to the level where HR becomes notified. Those thorny issues could have easily been resolved in the moment but now have grown by major proportions as more fuel is fed onto the fire. By the time lawyers come in to resolve the situation, people's livelihoods are at risk, not to mention the reputations of the involved parties and the company itself being sullied.

Your and your manager's ability to help the issue remain small and/or be resolved to everyone's satisfaction is a welcomed resource for HR. The HR team is a more helpful and willing ally once your conflict resolution competence is recognized.

Internal Customers and Suppliers

Most departments in any organization depend upon the work of people in other departments or other locations. And so much friction is created between departments. Books and articles abound on the problem of *silos* (Silo Syndrome) in a company. It is a natural defense mechanism to protect our turf, but most of the bad blood between departments is often due to a lack of communication. Let's start with these two questions:

1. What departments receive the product of your work? These are your internal customers, first and foremost.

2. What work product do you receive from other departments? These are your internal suppliers.

Your internal suppliers and customers are both sides of your team's ability to get the work done. When unacceptable product arrives from your internal supplier, the quality and timeliness of your department's output suffers. When your department provides incomplete or incorrect work product to the next department, it often needs to be re-worked, forms may need to be completed, or the product may need to be sent back to your department to be fixed.

Without timely and constructive feedback, the supplying department is unaware of the mistakes. Even worse, they have no idea just how frustrating receiving their sloppy work is for your team.

Example #1: The therapy department decided they needed to change the session timing to accommodate the therapist assistant schedules. It was only a thirty-minute change in the timing, so they instituted this great idea without delay. No big deal, right? Wrong!

The dietary department started receiving complaints the meals were cold when the patients got to their rooms. The dietary department's satisfaction scores tanked.

The nursing department's schedules were thrown off. Many patients had restrictions about taking their medication either with food or without food.

The counseling department had recurring meetings scheduled back to back. Their schedule was completely disrupted when the patients were either off to therapy or in the middle of their meals.

Example #2: Accounting versus sales. This seems to be a universal conflict and trigger point for disputes and hard feelings no matter the company or industry.

The accounting employees were held in low esteem by the sales department. The sales team members were always waiting through several pay cycles for their commission checks! The sales employees had developed inventive names for some of the accounting team members. Several felt the whole accounting department was jealous of how much money sales made and were delaying their money on purpose, just for spite.

The accounting team reviled the sales team members. Accounting described them as money grubbers, bullies, A-holes. Salespersons were calling and harassing the accounting employees every payday, demanding to know where their money was. Veiled threats were issued. Worse, when accounting tried to explain by phone what they needed from sales to close the deal, they were ignored.

In example #1, the therapy management's unawareness of their internal customers'/suppliers' needs caused the disastrous communication fail. Here is where the Law of Unintended Consequences lives. Part of developing any change is to bring everyone it may affect into the conversation.

In example #2, sales needs accounting to close the deals quickly, but accounting cannot close the deals without the complete information and paperwork it is sales' job to provide. In addition to failing to walk in each other's shoes, these two personality types often just do not understand each other. People with personalities who are drawn into sales tend to be more relationship driven. They paint broad brushstrokes instead of details and have an outgoing and expressive nature. Conversely, accounting attracts people of a reserved, quiet nature who have a laser-minded focus on details. (See Chapter 8: Personality Styles)

When two very different people work together on developing clear communication, there can be an armistice in hostilities and a reconciliation in understanding each other's needs. Our self-talk may go something like this: "It isn't important to me, and I don't understand why it is so important to her, but now I do understand it is. That's enough 'why' for me."

Other Employees

Taking the heat and calming the drama

Just by increasing your awareness and observation skills, you will start seeing small irritations well before even the parties involved do.

"Joe just snapped my head off—what the heck was that all about?"

"Mary just called"—big sigh—"she's going to be a few minutes late…again."

"Why does Jane get to wear sandals? What makes her so special she doesn't have to meet the dress code?"

"Sammy forgot to lock the door again. I think he just wants to be fired!"

In all these cases, something in the team member's personal health or life is affecting them at work. The fallout from not addressing the behaviors causing these comments will just add more and more frustration on both sides.

Letting Joe know he's especially grumpy today helps him realize to take a break and tone it down.

Asking if you can help Mary make it to work on time alerts her others are noticing.

Jane may value her privacy and certainly does not need to discuss her ADA accommodation with her co-workers, but she needs to know others are wondering.

Sammy's forgetfulness or distraction in his rush to get to personal commitments is putting the company's security at risk. He might not even know he didn't lock the door!

Each of these situations also represents an opportunity for some creative solutions!

Practice Tips

These great tips I've started practicing come from Vanessa Van Edwards' book *Captivate*. Try these out when the person you are with is upset.

First, do NOT EVER say "Calm down" in any way, shape, or form! All it does is to further entrench the person into the matter at hand. Remember, the issue/person bothering her is *important to her*. It may be trivial in your mind, or she may just be wrong in her beliefs, but telling anyone to "calm down" just shuts down her ears, entrenches the problem in her mind, and destroys your opportunity to help her.

So, what do you say? Nothing. Ask what is wrong and LISTEN. Let her talk it out.

I know—you are busy and you don't have time for this. Here's the question, though: How much time and how many future interruptions will there be if you cannot help her resolve her emotions now?

If the situation involves a subordinate or a customer complaint, then pull out a note pad and jot down notes.

Ask clarifying questions. This helps her clear her mind and express her thoughts.

Use the Six Sigma technique—'The 5 Whys.' If you're not familiar with it, just Google it. There's a wealth of information on this tool.

Repeat the words of concern they use in response to your questions. By you responding back with words describing her concern, she instinctively feels you are actively listening to her.

> When she uses an emotionally charged word or phrase, let her hear it back from you. This causes them to re-assess the term and often will cause them to re-think the situation more logically.

When emotions get involved, people often jump to the worst-case scenario. It may have felt like the other person was yelling at her but really wasn't even raising their voice.

I had a new employee complain her manager was "harassing" her. She was in tears and displaying a victim mentality. However, when I repeated the emotional trigger word back to her, she looked at me thoughtfully, paused, then said he wasn't really harassing her, but he was being mean and demanding.

It turns out she was not yet competent and probably would not even be capable of performing the job. Of course she felt vulnerable! The manager was frustrated and known for his short temper. I could just imagine the interaction causing her to come to HR.

Outcome? She took the rest of the day off. The manager had already documented the training, her continued poor performance, and necessary re-training. The next day, she called me. When she got home, she had come to realize the job wasn't in her skill set and she was going back to her previous employer. She even thanked me for taking my time to listen and to understand her.

Chapter Summary/Key Takeaways

Our ability to work across departmental lines involves good communication and an understanding of how the quality of our work affects others.

Active listening is the key to keeping small problems small, friction to a minimum, and emotional drama reduced. Just by lending an ear, we have a huge impact on others. It lets others know we appreciate their contribution and are willing to help.

In the next chapter, we will see how we affect many others outside the company, too.

Chapter 6: Other Stakeholders

We never get a second chance to make a good first impression.
We always get the next chance to enforce, improve, or destroy
first impressions, though.

Customers and End Users

Everything done at work affects the end user in some way. Attention to detail helps ensure quality. Attention to function, fit, and fashion makes all the difference in the way the customer experiences your product. Attention to production time and keeping waste and re-work down affects the pricing of your product. Attention to treating all in a respectful, thoughtful manner in person and through media affects the customer's perception and the reputation of your product and the company as a whole.

Yes, *your* product! You may never touch or see the end product, but you are a part of crafting the customer's experience of it.

A very few companies really adopt this into the core of their being. Some of the most highly valued brands are examples of this. Their CEOs are household names and carry the company's banner of a high-quality, reputable organization.

I've noticed, though, the people who are the company's workforce have the most direct and immediate impact on the customer. The sloppily placed label, the missing assembly piece, the wrinkled seam—all have an effect on the customer's perception of quality. Of course, those interpersonal contacts with employees create the most visceral and memorable reactions customers have.

One of my favorite stories is about an elderly customer who had just visited the store. When she tried to leave, her car would not start. One of the lawn-maintenance people noticed and offered to help. He ran inside, asked for jumper cables, then returned to the lady's car, opening the hood and chatting with her for the short while it took for an employee to appear with a portable charger. As the car started, she profusely thanked the lawn-maintenance man and the other employee.

The next day, the lady posted a kudos and thank-you in the sound-off section of the newspaper, and her daughter posted an extremely positive message on her social media pages about the wonderful customer service. What great press! And the kicker is that the lawn guy did not work for the store at all. He worked for the shopping center. However, he'd had positive interactions with several of the store's employees and wanted to help them take care of their customer.

Remember: We never get a second chance to make a good first impression. We always get the next chance to enforce, improve, or destroy first impressions, though.

Vendors and Suppliers

Do you have a vendor who is just irritating your team to the max? As an example: your company's coffee-service vendor sends out new delivery people every few weeks. Situations include not bringing the right products, leaving the boxes and trash in the cafeteria room, parking the delivery truck where it blocks the customer drive-through, and being generally rude or unresponsive to requests.

So, you may wonder, why does the company still use this vendor?! Is it price? How much time, effort, and aggravation are they causing your team? The purchasing department may have no idea there is any problem.

Does your manager even know about the chaos these perpetually new, untrained delivery people cause? Wouldn't your manager like to be the hero to your team by replacing this vendor with a competent one?!

You could make it happen!

Practice Tip

Find out who oversees purchasing this service. If not your manager, then your manager could ask some of these questions:

–What are the consequences of changing/not changing the company?

–Are we their best customer?

–Do they value our account?

--What's the best way to approach the buyer? You never know—the supplier may be the owner's brother-in-law.

--What could you do, or how could you aid your manager in correcting the problem?

By the same token, your suppliers and vendors have a vested interest in the success of your department and the company as a whole. If your design department has a successful roll-out of a new product using parts from company A, company A enjoys the extra sales, too! If your company is in a growth phase due to the increased productivity and profits from its well-run departments, building additional workspace will utilize several different suppliers, from the construction phase, to the outfitting of equipment, to the furnishings. Even your company's payroll processor will enjoy increased revenue as your company adds employees to the staff.

The Community and Region

The ripple effects are felt far and wide when any change occurs. It really becomes obvious when an unexpected event or explosive growth happens. We saw the trickle-down effect most drastically in our community during the Great Recession starting in 2008.

During that time, a large employer suddenly shut its doors without warning. The customers were left hanging, and employees were in shock. The local state employment-service office was swamped with unemployment claims; the local staffing agencies were inundated with résumés; the coffee-services supplier and the package delivery company both laid off full-time employees due to the huge drop in business from this one customer. The local charitable organizations, already stretched thin, were called upon to serve more who were in critical need. The local banks soon were sending out past-due notices on unpaid monthly debt payments. Even today, many young adults still carry the scars from when their families were thrown into crisis mode.

Now in 2019, we are still experiencing the effects in our area from the last few years of explosive commercial construction growth. Suppliers are raising prices, suffering material shortages, and adding staffing to keep pace with the demand. The smaller contractors and subcontractors are having to adjust their prices and are finding it difficult to compete with the big guys for qualified talent.

Chapter Summary/Key Takeaways

We are all performing work that matters to others. What I see, though, is many employees and managers not recognizing just how important their contributions really are to others! When our work group realizes our work affects everyone around us, even those out into our community and the world, it changes attitudes, makes the work atmosphere more positive, and improves communications and relationships.

Our fellow employees, other departments, customers, and end users, even our suppliers and vendors, benefit from or are negatively affected by how we do our work. Whether big or small, our company's success or failure has a direct impact on the health of our communities.

In the next chapter, you will learn about: What is in it for the company? This is where the argument for investing in changes can be quantified.

Chapter 7: The Company

If senior management/C-suite can see the potential upside to making changes and to investing in innovative ideas for improvement, they can move mountains. However, it often takes arguments with provable data to convince the folks at the top to approve big initiatives.

The two major areas where you can find data to support your manager's proposal for improvement are all tied back to these:

1. Customers and Reputation

Reputation and word-of-mouth have never been as important as today to a company's bottom line in this age of social media. I will bet there is an amazing amount of data the company already gathers in this area. Basics I can think of off the top of my head are:

- Product returns

- Complaints

- Distributor volume

- Standing in the marketplace

- Positive/negative reviews

- News media attention

Your manager or her manager will have access to the data. Great customer service team members will know these numbers and trendlines as well. Unfortunately, managers often fail to see the forest for the trees. Just by mentioning the possible downline consequences helps your manager consider more of the repercussions of her decisions.

2. Profits and Growth

While a rising tide lifts all boats, a low tide will strand or ground most of those boats in the sand. While not all growth is profitable, growing profits increase amazing opportunities for the company's future. Some places to look for increasing profits include:

- Reducing inventory turns

- Reducing time to make

- Increasing sales

- Increasing marketing effectiveness

- Reducing re-work and waste

- Reducing overhead

- Increasing customer retention

- Increasing employee Retention

Having access to and using these figures helps quantify possible scenarios. Just use the formulae:

- If we increase X by Y%, it will add Z$.

- If we reduce X by Y%, it will save us Z$.

The company who looks for and encourages employees' and managers' ideas will try out things in a beta test. This is part of the great strategy Jim Collins explains in his book, *Good to Great.*

If the Proposed Change Is Too Drastic for Your Manager to Get Full Approval

The senior team has probably done a quick cost/benefit analysis, along with analyzing possible consequences, and doesn't see enough upside to risk the changes needed. You could be facing these roadblocks:

- Your manager's manager does not believe it will work.

- She doesn't care enough about the idea to invest any time or effort to implement.

- She doesn't have the authority to implement without approval from her manager.

You may be able to overcome objections by proposing a beta test to try the idea. This also helps by using the results to work the kinks out before a full implementation. This is also the way to turn theory into the verifiable data senior management crave.

Many Changes Don't NEED Approval!

HOWEVER, your company *already* benefits from so many small changes implemented day to day, process by process, without *any* approval from anyone!

- The technician's process shaves time off replacing or installing a part and *also* makes it safer.

- The admin assistant's filing process tweak reduces error rates.

- The shipper who has figured out how to palletize a load faster and more securely speeds up delivery times and reduces damaged freight showing up at the customer's door.

These are your department's thinkers and innovators. If your manager is already recognizing them and having them mentor and train their process to others, great! If not, she's missing a fabulous resource and opportunity.

This is where building a relationship with other supervisors can really pay off for you, your manager, and the company. Here are some possibilities:

- Facilities maintenance is having problems with some equipment. The tech on your work team has some ideas.

- Sales is just terrible at completing paperwork accurately and on time. A project including one or two from each department could develop an easy checklist the sales team will appreciate and actually follow.

Documentation

"If it isn't documented, it wasn't done!" HR and safety departments preach this mantra over and over. Why? Because employees, departments, and companies are doing most things *right*! By not documenting their work, they just aren't taking credit for it!

The company benefits every day from small incremental improvements their employees make to their processes. Does your senior management team know all the good things going on in your work unit? Does your manager even know?

Here's another phrase for those who hesitate to blow their own horn: ***"It's not bragging if it is true!"***

Practice Tip

Think about your work team. Who on the team is an expert craftsperson? Who on the team has lengthy experience on the job? Who is always thinking of new ideas?

Now, are there any processes they have already improved based on their input? Is there a current snag or frustrating task one or more of them may be able to help figure out?

Wouldn't it be great if the company recognized those star performers in the newsletter? And a thank-you by your manager's manager is always an amazing morale booster.

Chapter Summary/Key Takeaways

Your manager and her team gain credibility with the higher-ups as more positive news is fed their way. The more they hear good things coming out of the department, the more likely they will be inclined to try larger and more companywide initiatives!

In the next chapter, we will get to know your manager better to understand just why she does and says the things she does.

PART III: Who Is Your Manager?

"One size does not fit all."

For the purposes of this book, we are talking mainly of the person you directly report to. In some businesses, especially small ones, you may actually report to more than one person. For simplicity's sake, let's define this person as the one who:

- Is next in the business hierarchy,

- Has a superior who gets the benefit of their work, and

- Is the person you most interact with on a daily and weekly basis.

Chapter 8: Personality

We are all wired so differently!

Knowing your manager's personality style can help you predict her response or reaction to different stimuli at work. Understanding the basic styles really helps us understand our "What were they thinking?!" moments.

Figuring out someone's basic personality style is easy with the many different assessments available today. I've used DiSC, Wired That Way, Myers Briggs, Predictive Index, Scarf360, and Enneagram. They all have their strengths. Pricing can range from as low as free versions on the internet to over $200 for a comprehensive report. The more comprehensive ones break down personalities into upwards of 16 types.

My personal favorites of the style assessments are Disc or Wired That Way. Each divides the primary and secondary personality preferences into four quadrants and uses the same color scheme. Wired That Way is simpler and less costly yet still gives a general picture of the person's personality. This graphic gives us a summary of the four basic personality styles. (Refer to Chapter 5 for examples of different personality styles in action.)

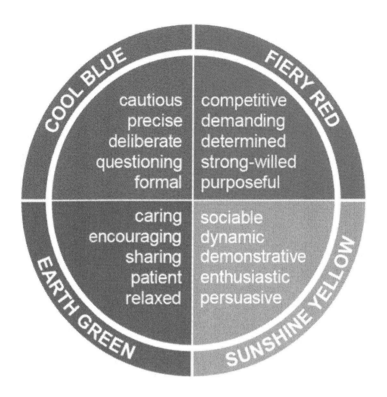

Just by looking at these descriptive words, you can probably pick out friends and family who fall into each of these quadrants. The most recent statistics I found show as of 2013 the United States profile distributions were: (Courtesy of: www.johnruh.com/global-disc-behavioral-profiles-research-statistics/)

- 17% of the population have the **"D" Dominant** style of *Red*

- 38% of the population skew toward the *Yellow* **"I" Influencing** style

- 32% are in the **"S" <u>Steady</u>** *Green* quadrant

- And only 13% are in the **"C" <u>Conscientious</u>** *Blue* quadrant

Without overanalyzing your boss, can you pick out which primary color she might belong in?

As a "C" I suffer from Analysis Paralysis. It's one reason why I am so familiar with all these different assessment instruments. I can study and wade into details to the point I will not make a decision! As we see below, this is a common problem with the "C" or blue-colored personality style found in several assessments.

Often our personalities include a secondary color as well. We will most often see the two are either side by side or top and bottom on this graph. The top half, Red and Blue, is more TASK oriented. The bottom half, Green and Yellow, is more RELATIONSHIP oriented. Can you see how a manager (Red) may not understand the devastating impact her harsh word has on a (Green) subordinate?

On the left side, Blue and Green are more INTROVERTED. Red & Yellow on the left are more

EXTROVERTED. Can you see how a supervisor (Blue) might not understand why cancelling the holiday party has the whole sales department (Yellow) in an uproar?

Your manager views her world through the lens of her personality style. Just knowing this about her is an especially important start in decoding why she does, says, and thinks the way she does!

For me, realizing so many people think and react completely differently than I do was a complete shock! Now, I take it in stride and do a better job communicating by keeping the other person's personality cues in mind.

Practice Tip

See if you can figure out which one or two colors best describe your manager. Find out if your manager is familiar with personality assessments. If so, ask her what personality she thinks you are. This gets the conversation going about the other personalities on the team. If she is not familiar with the assessments, encourage her to take one. How? It depends of course on HER personality style! Here are some talking tips by color:

YELLOW: "There's a fun version on line. Super easy and really helped me relate to my friends better. Wanna' try it?"

BLUE: "There is a really detailed version on line. It's free. I was surprised how accurate and simple the test was. I wonder how much more informative the full-featured one is."

GREEN: "There is a really clear version on line I shared with my _____. We have really grown our relationship because of it."

RED: "The quick version on line gets to the point without all the fluff. It really helped me compete on a different level with my _____ group."

Chapter Summary/Key Takeaways

Unless your manager has participated in a personality assessment, she is more than likely oblivious to the stark differences in how we each perceive and react to our world. She probably is often surprised at the reaction she receives from people and how differently her words and intentions are interpreted.

Understanding her personality style helps start hinting at why she does, says, thinks, acts, and reacts in particular ways to people and events throughout the day.

In the next chapter, we will start figuring out what is important to her.

Chapter 9: What Is Important to Your Manager?

"Next to physical survival, the greatest need of a human being is psychological survival – to be understood, to be affirmed, to be validated, to be appreciated."–Stephen Covey

We are a product of striving to satisfy both survival needs in Mr. Covey's quote above. In the world of work, physical survival is covered by a living wage and good safety controls. The psychological needs are just as important to survival and even more important to the company's productivity, and to the individual's self-worth and drive for success.

Maslow's Hierarchy of needs

When we understand where we are on the pyramid, we can avoid misinterpreting others' motivations by our standards.

Maslow's hierarchy of needs is a theory proposed by Abraham Maslow in his 1943 paper "A Theory of Human Motivation" in *Psychological Review*.

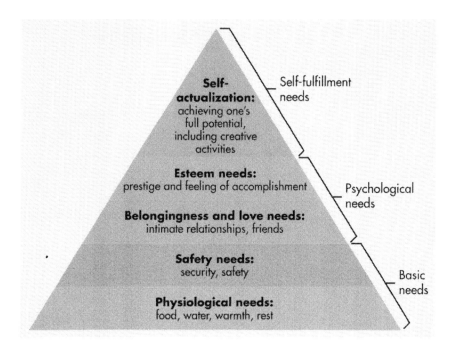

Yes, it has been around for nearly eighty years and is still a crucial part of advertising and marketing plans, benefits-and-rewards packages, and general motivational strategies.

So, where is your manager on Maslow's pyramid? Let's look at a few different scenarios. Where would you guess these managers might fit on the scale?

- Newly promoted twenty-something with college loans and a new baby.

- Micromanager who comes in early and stays late. Known for taking credit and bragging about successes.

- Long-timer with the company who seems to be 'phoning it in.'

- Office is decorated with framed photos of manager with celebrities, certificates, and awards.

- Organizes events and enjoys coordinating the softball team.

"I've noticed my own degree of focus on the particular needs levels fluctuates as my time and circumstances change."

Yes, your manager may have an upcoming expense or a medical emergency knocking her down the list for a while. However, the more we experience the fulfillment of the higher-level needs, the less stressful a temporary dip down the pyramid usually is.

By the way...where are YOU focusing your efforts within this hierarchy?

Practice Tip

Is your manager familiar with Maslow's hierarchy? Unless your company is fanatical about training managers, maybe not. Ask the question.

Refer back to the Personality Wheel and use it to influence your approach based on her dominant personality.

- If your manager has BLUE in her personality, she will be curious and want to analyze the team using the hierarchy's details.

- If your manager has RED in her personality, she will use this as a shortcut to making decisions.

- If your manager has GREEN in her personality, she will want the crew members to get the help they need.

- And if your manager has YELLOW in her personality style, she will use it in promoting her agendas to others.

Values

Definition: Important and lasting beliefs or ideals shared by the members of a culture about what is good or bad and desirable or undesirable. Values have major influence on a person's behavior and attitude and serve as broad guidelines in all situations. Some common business values are fairness, innovation, and community involvement. http://www.businessdictionary.com/definition/values.html

Businesses say they have values, and we've seen the values plastered on the walls and printed in the marketing collateral. Yet we do not see those values practiced in the day-to-day operations. One reason is that people have differing values and sometimes even conflicting values.

Personal values do not change quickly or sometimes ever. They are the bedrock of who we are and what we think. They guide our actions and define our attitudes and perceptions of what we experience and who we interact with.

But ask anyone what their values are, and few will be able to say them clearly, quickly, or concisely. It isn't hard to think of some words to express our values. The challenge is narrowing down the words into four or five best-defining terms.

As you can see below, there is an amazing array of words to select from in creating a Values Statement.

If your company has a list of values, great. Chances are some of those values don't show on our or our manager's list, though.

VALUES EXERCISE

This is a fabulous exercise! I suggest you try it!

To determine your core values (adapted from Taproot): from the list below, choose <u>every</u> core value you like. Do not overthink your selections! There are over 120, so you'll have between 15 and 40 to begin with.

Now sort your list into 4 to 6 columns of words belonging together (i.e. Grace with Selflessness or Fun with Playfulness)

PICK the Best word in each of the new lists and add a verb to it! BOOM—*you have your list of Core Values!*

Abundance	Benevolence	Cooperation
Acceptance	Boldness	Collaboration
Accountability	Brilliance	Consistency
Achievement	Calmness	Contribution
Adventure	Caring	Creativity
Advocacy	Challenge	Credibility
Ambition	Charity	Curiosity
Appreciation	Cheerfulness	Daring
Attractiveness	Cleverness	Decisiveness
Autonomy	Community	Dedication
Balance	Commitment	Dependability
Being the Best	Compassion	Diversity

How to Train Your Manager

Effecting Change	Individuality	Power
Empathy	Innovation	Preparedness
Encouragement	Inspiration	Proactive
Enthusiasm	Intelligence	Professionalism
Ethics	Intuition	Punctuality
Excellence	Joy	Quality
Expressiveness	Kindness	Recognition
Fairness	Knowledge	Risk Taking
Family	Leadership	Safety
Friendships	Learning	Security
Flexibility	Love	Service
Freedom	Loyalty	Spirituality
Fun	Mindfulness	Stability
Generosity	Motivation	Relationships
Grace	Optimism	Reliability
Growth	Open-Mindedness	Resilience
Flexibility	Originality	Resourcefulness
Happiness	Passion	Responsibility
Health	Peace	Responsiveness
Honesty	Perfection	Security
Humility	Performance	Self-Control
Humor	Personal Growth	Selflessness
Inclusiveness	Playfulness	Simplicity
Independence	Popularity	Stability

Success	Understanding	Wealth
Teamwork	Uniqueness	Well-Being
Thankfulness	Usefulness	Wisdom
Thoughtfulness	Versatility	Zeal
Traditionalism	Vision	
Trustworthiness	Warmth	

Wouldn't it be illuminating to discover your manager's core values? What words on this list already come to mind when thinking about her?

I worked for one manager who demanded loyalty and would feel betrayed personally when others acted contrary to her wishes. When I advocated for a win-win solution, she believed it would cause her to lose face!

She told me I was being "disloyal" to her! After nursing my wounded ego for a day, I went back and framed how the solution WAS demonstrating my loyalty to the company and by extension to her as well.

Another manager I worked with craved autonomy. She wouldn't consider other ideas once she had created a plan of action in her mind. Once, when the ownership sent down an accounting change, she refused to institute it although the change didn't really affect the operations at our level. It turned out she had created the system they were replacing!

I quickly learned the best way to have things approved by her was to coach her into discovering the solution herself.

Chapter Summary/Key Takeaways

We are all driven by physical and psychological needs. Just knowing where we and others are on Maslow's hierarchy and what all our core values are gives us amazing insight into ourselves and how others tick.

In the next chapter, we will see behaviors are the clues we need to understand her perceptions on penalties and rewards.

Chapter 10: Behaviors

"All behavior is a function of its consequences—you get what you reward."–Bob Nelson

Behavior definitions run the gamut from simple to extremely complex. Synonyms include conduct, demeanor, performance, comportment, actions, and deeds. So instead of getting bogged down in the semantics, let's just look at two areas where a manager displays her behaviors.

What Is She Good At?

Here are ways we can view repetitive behaviors resulting, at least in her mind, in a positive outcome. Let's examine these two scenarios.

Scenario #1: I had a manager who was extremely punctual and prompt in meeting goals and deadlines. It was so important to her that the work sometimes suffered. Her subordinates often experienced her displeasure and harsh reprimands when they did not meet her sometimes unreasonable expectations.

Scenario #2: I knew a foreperson who loved organizing events! It could be as simple as celebrating someone's birthday or as complex as putting together and running a bowling league. Her main topic of conversation was generally about her latest event planning, so her co-workers knew her focus was not on the office. They often supervised the work by committee without her input.

In both these scenarios, we can clearly see their strengths by observing where they place their attention and focus. Here are some questions you can ask to tease out less obvious skills and passions:

What books/articles does she read or podcasts does she listen to?

What are her hobbies and preferred non-work activities? What non-work groups does she belong to? Does she travel, spend time with family, or volunteer at some charitable organization?

Where Does She Need Help?

As you can see above, sometimes answering those questions can reveal her areas where she could use improvement.

We all have our blind spots. Here is where your help can really propel her performance into high gear and improve your relationships along the way.

Example: I am NOT time aware at all. Not long after receiving my first smart phone, my assistant showed me how to set reminders on my calendar and alarms on my clock apps. Was she just being helpful, or did those apps relieve her from having to constantly find me and remind me when my presence was required elsewhere?

By finding where your manager focuses her energies, we can start to see the clues to answering the next question.

What Is Her Perceived Reward?

This is the real question. The reward we are driving for is often unconscious and unexamined. For some, it takes years of therapy to tease out the hidden motivations driving our actions. Most of us aren't psychologists or mind readers, but by looking at our values, needs, personality style, talents, and where we struggle, we can get at least a general picture.

Here's another exercise…

Manager 1: She's been with the same company for over twenty years. She doesn't belong to groups and either does not attend company parties or if she shows, she pays her respects, stands in the background, and leaves early.

Her work is detailed and thorough. Colleagues have never seen her upset or getting into an argument. Her office is purely functional with a photo of her pet as her only personal item. She hasn't taken a vacation, other than a long weekend here and there, in years. She dresses conservatively. Only HR has any idea of her marital status.

- What values might she choose?

- What personality profile fits her best?

- How does she display her talents?

- Where is she in Maslow's hierarchy?

- What situations are uncomfortable for her?

Now, think of how her behaviors make her feel fulfilled.

Manager 2: She's been with the company for several years. She's a sports fan, organizes the football pool, and has a group of fans and alumni she hangs out with. Her office is adorned with memorabilia, including photos of her with various sports celebrities. She drives a motorcycle to work when weather allows. She's unmarried, has no kids, and uses most of her vacation time to travel to sporting events all over the country.

- What values might she choose?

- What personality profile fits her best?

- Where are her talents?

- Where is she in Maslow's hierarchy?

- What situations are uncomfortable for her?

Now, think of how her behaviors make her feel fulfilled.

Yes, I agree, this is a guessing game, but as you can see, there are definite clues. Each manager's behaviors are driven by her need to be satisfied, pleased, and rewarded. Knowing this helps frame our conversations toward satisfying her underlying reward needs.

I had a manager who wanted to buy event tickets for a goal completion. The thing was, very few if any of the team members were interested in the event. The manager absolutely was, though, and automatically thought everyone else would love to be able to go, too.

Another manager wanted to give away extra PTO days as a reward to a team who refused to use their regular allotment of time-off days. In fact, most lost the left-over days every anniversary.

The reward needs to fit the person's interest. Understanding her intrinsic reward desires helps us understand why a person places certain values on the many pieces of the workplace tasks-and-relationship puzzle.

Limiting Beliefs

When I learned about limiting beliefs, it changed my life. I had lived in the comfort zone of my limiting beliefs for years. Suddenly, I was hearing my own beliefs were keeping me from being successful, were holding me back from trying new things and achieving more.

Limiting beliefs come from stories we tell ourselves— negative comments we've heard from others, cultural norms we were raised in, and our justifications of failures in our past. We hear those limiting beliefs as negative self-talk we tell ourselves and hear from others.

I had a supervisor who bemoaned the fact he hadn't gone to college. When the chance for a promotion came, he didn't even apply for the opening! I felt he was the best person for the job. He had the experience, knew the work and the people, was organized, and had those wonderful people skills so needed in the workplace.

We promoted him anyway as interim. Unfortunately, he floundered in the new position. He was flustered and unsure of himself. He dragged his feet on decisions as production of the unit tanked. He admitted he wasn't sleeping well. He was timid in meetings.

Finally, we moved him back to the supervisor position when we found a highly qualified candidate. Seemingly overnight, he changed back to the proficient manager we knew him to be. Soon, we sent him to a management training course provided by the local community college. With that certificate, he was able to overcome his limiting belief and applied for the next management opening.

Limiting beliefs are the beliefs holding us back. Evidence of limiting beliefs include:

- Negative self-talk. "That's not me." "You're so lucky." "I could never do that." "I'm not [strong, smart, brave] enough."

- Cultural norms: "In my family, we are (or we don't) _____."

- FEAR (false evidence appearing real): "We tried it before, and it was a disaster." "That's too risky." "Kid, you'll shoot your eye out."

Rules vs. Expectations

Did you know negative statements do not register in our brains? The often-repeated example is: Do NOT think of a pink elephant in the room. Of course, most of us at once imagine a pink elephant! Changing the statement to: Do think of an empty room. Result: Elephant image disappears.

If your manager tends to focus on the negatives as a way to drive performance, you have a huge opportunity! Just phrasing the same issue to explain the positive outcome desired changes everything. It is really the difference between rules and expectations in the workplace.

Rules have consequences, implied or actual.

- Don't be late again or…

- Quit talking and get back to work or …

- No more personal phone calls or…

- If I catch you without your hard hat again...

Expectations have standards to meet.

- We expect you to be at your desk five minutes before start of shift.

- We expect you to use your breaks for personal calls. Of course, if there is an emergency, leave our main phone number so we can get you immediately.

- We expect you to stay at your work station and limit your conversations to work-related matters while you are on the clock.

- We expect you to comply with all our safety procedures, including wearing your hard hat on site.

A-Holes Versus Narcissists

We keep hearing the word *narcissist* these days when discussions are referring to a boss, an ex-, or some other jerk. Most of the time, the person being discussed has just showed his or her A-hole, jerk, butt-head, and SOB side. Those and other terms help describe selfish, egotistical, and uncaring behaviors reflecting poorly on the offender.

However, there ARE bosses out there who fit the clinical diagnosis of Narcissist Personality Disorder (NPD), though fortunately those are few and far between. We need to know the difference! I found this great nine-point comparison on Lisa Thompson's website: www.lisathomsonlive.com. Please check it out for more details and examples. Here are the points summarized:

- Narcissists love to *gaslight* (manipulate others into questioning their own sanity). A-holes light their own fires.

- Narcissists never apologize. A-holes love to apologize.

- Narcissists know what they want and how to get it. Rules don't apply to narcissists. A-holes understand the difference between right and wrong.

- Narcissists never go too far to get what they want. A-holes know when to quit. They are capable of knowing when they've gone too far.

- Narcissists are among the most charming people you will ever meet. A-holes are not charming.

- Narcissists are superficial. A-holes have deep thoughts and analytic capability.

- Narcissists play the role of 'victim.' A-holes rarely act like victims.

- Narcissists are habitual liars, twisting facts to suit their reputation. A-holes don't habitually lie to get their way.

- Narcissists are socially insatiable. They can never get enough attention. A-holes often enjoy time alone and don't feel insecure about their solitude.

If your manager shows A-hole behavior, she is probably coachable and often knows what she did or said was 'just wrong.'

But if your manager has Narcissistic Personality Disorder, it is time to dust off your résumé and get away. There is nothing you can do to change her or help her, and you will just be a pawn in her game, so get out. Get out *now*.

Chapter Summary/Key Takeaways

Our manager shows her colors in many ways by giving us glimpses of who she is and what motivates her. When we have better insight, we can better understand her motivations and emphasize with her driving needs and wants. We can be an extra set of eyes and ears to uncover her blind spots and make for a more well-rounded view of the situation, the players, and the environment.

In the next chapter, we will start learning how to implement our plan of action...

PART IV: Implementation

"Never let the thought of weakness enter your consciousness, but always ignore the suggestion and affirm yourself to be the tower of strength, within and without."–Charles Fillmore

Chapter 11: How to Be Heard!

I've read many entrepreneurs and high achievers are ADHD ("squirrel"). This manager requires a manager to keep her from rabbit-trailing off topic. How do we influence her without insulting, badgering, or parenting?

Being the Manager Trainer is a skill learned by trial and error. This is not a one-size-fits-all formula, but several things can work for most personality types.

More Gets Caught Than Taught

Being an example of how to do it right is often effective. Heaven knows it worked when your manager parrots and imitates her first authority figures! Children learn how to do so many things just by watching the big people. Sometimes we catch ourselves repeating to our kids those memorable phrases our parents drummed into us as we grew.

The hitch to this is we are not your manager's authority figure. Why would she even pay attention when you are showing the kind of behavior you want her to emulate? The trick is to get her attention.

Practice Tip

Try this: Ask your manager to help you. Tell her you would like her feedback after watching you or your team interacting with others.

If instead you told her to "watch and learn," it is likely she would dismiss your input and even reprimand you for rudeness. But by asking her to help you with this situation as you are learning to handle it, she will be interested, involved, and feel respected as your superior. Plus, she may learn something she can apply to her leadership skills!

It takes a little planning but can be so effective. Try it!

Sound Bites, Nibbles, and Whispers in Her Ear

Ego Continuum

STRONG--fragile

If your manager falls to either extreme on this Ego Continuum, she does not want to hear your ideas.

Managers with strong egos think they already have the answer. Managers with fragile egos will interpret suggestions and offered ideas as threats to their position or even identity.

How can we coach her without risking the relationship and possibly our own job?

It is a little tricky, but feeding the idea to her in small bits often works over time. The goal is to let the idea slowly trickle into her subconscious so she will think of it as her own! This method takes patience, stealth, and a swallowing of our own ego. "It is the result that counts" was my mantra when applying this technique.

In one scenario, the manager's complaint is that it costs too much and takes too long to train new hires for certification. "Once they get certified, they are going to leave anyway." However, Tommy already works for you.

"Too bad training takes so long."

"That kid (referring to Tom) would be perfect if he just had his certification."

"It sure is hard to find qualified help these days."

"There was an article in the paper today about Company X getting a training grant..."

These are some examples of comments thrown in during conversations in front of the manager over a period of four or more weeks.

Caution: Making these comments too frequently, especially in front of others in the chain of command, can backfire. *Remember: patience and stealth.* The goal is for her to connect the dots herself.

Understand you will never get the credit, but you and your team will enjoy the progress!

Learn Her Communication Preference

Do you know which method she works best with? The simplest way is to just ask her in a one-on-one conversation. "How do you like to be communicated with…email, text, face to face? With details? With bullet points?"

My friend had a boss who hated to read. Long emails were simply poison to her. A short email summarizing the issue with a request for a meeting was her preferred method of communication. Another of her managers NEVER wanted to talk with the team other than regularly scheduled staff meetings, so all communications needed to be fully explained in writing. The lesson here? adjust your communication style to your manager's preferences.

I had two fairly young, recently promoted managers who would not answer their phones or respond to my emails. It was SO FRUSTRATING! Fortunately for me, their offices were both close by, so I would include a stop to chat with them on my regular walks around the properties any time I needed a conversation with them. Finally, one of the new managers said, "But why didn't you just text me?"

I had to change MY preference for the sake of better and much quicker responses. I learned the text function on my phone. I also coached them to use professional language in their business communication texts. They had no idea texts ARE discoverable in lawsuits! It is worthwhile to screenshot ones involving serious issues as a method of CYA (covering your anatomy). Remember the sentence, "If it isn't documented, it isn't done."

Speak Her Language

Mirroring is a technique allowing others to feel more comfortable with you when you reply in a pace and style similar to their way of expressing themselves. Mirroring is easy to learn. The main skill is just to observe the person's style more intentionally. It does take a little practice, but it is a valuable skill worth learning.

The key is to not mimic or overdo it. Most people will feel you are making fun of them, especially when it comes to their personally identifiable traits such as accent, gestures, and other body language.

To start out, you already do this instinctively with people you've known for a long time and respect. Grandma takes a long time to spin her story and often pauses to stir her tea. A dutiful grandchild will mirror her tea preference and engage in the conversation of the long, drawn-out storyline.

Some other examples:

The professor. If you are a willing student, you are speaking her language here. She often has years of experience and expounds on examples, theories, and previous experiences to support her ideas and plans. If her conversations become long lectures, then it is time for you as a good student to guide the subject back to the matters at hand.

The slow talker. If you are from the Northeast USA, it might just irritate the snot out of you to try to get a thought out of her. Slow down; relax. This is her pace; mirror and work with it.

The fast talker. "Facts, just the facts, ma'am" is a famous line from an incredibly old detective show. "Get 'er done!" is often the fast talker's mantra. She may exhibit her speed in her speech pattern and/or in her decisive, impatient way of talking about the subject. This manager probably has a lot of Red in her personality profile. She will connect with you much better if you develop a way of speaking in headlines and broad brushstrokes. If she wants or needs details, she will ask for them. When she does ask, she wants to hear them immediately, so be ready. Long, drawn-out meetings make her antsy and irritated. Keep it short, and be prepared.

The long talker. Schedule for this meeting to take extra time. It is going to take longer. We need to allow her the time to work out her thoughts. Long talkers sometimes fall into the following sub-categories. It is worth discussing because if we learn more about WHY she takes so long, it is easier for us to adapt and to work with her.

- *The rabbit-trail talker.* She will often get off topic with her lateral ideas, but these can sometimes contain hidden gems. She often really needs this talking exercise to organize and plan. Don't be afraid to ask how the story relates to the topic. It will either pull her back from an unconnected story or, more often, she will explain how this unrelated experience or fact applies. You are actually helping by gifting your listening time to her.

- *The lonely gal.* Managers are often the loneliest people in the building. This is especially true if her personality is Yellow or Green. She is starved for collegial conversations and has found in you someone she feels comfortable with.

- *The former teammate*. DANGER: You used to be co-workers and friends. Now she's your boss, but you and she value your friendship. Yes, you could be the "boss whisperer" to her, but your relationship appears to others as an example of favoritism. This is a disaster waiting to happen to both your futures. The best remedies are:

  A. Agree to put the friendship on the shelf. No more off-work meets or personal relationship at all. Become colleagues and friendly, but no longer friends. Others in the department and company will notice and most likely will respect your professional approach.

  B. Decide the friendship is more important. One of you will need to transfer departments or leave the organization. It will most likely happen anyway, and it is only a matter of time before your relationship causes one or both of your positions to be at risk. Years ago, against my better judgment, I hired my best friend to work in the department then later had to fire her. It destroyed our relationship, and I regret losing her friendship to this day.

- *The new person on the team*. Getting to know the new boss is exactly what this book is about! Use the tools to help her integrate into the position and smooth the way for your, her, and the team's success. She will definitely need a sounding board. It might as well be you. DANGER: For your future and hers, this relationship must stay collegial and not evolve into friendship until you are no longer in the same chain of command. I have several great friends now who were at one time my employees. It wasn't until after we were no longer working together that we moved from colleagues to friend status.

- *The "lost in the details" talker.* Managers need to be decisive, and those of us who suffer from 'analysis paralysis' often try to talk the problem to death. Why? We think the answer is just one more piece of information away. Help her to define the best of an imperfect solution. Remind her that not deciding IS making a decision! Looking at the situation from another viewpoint helps in most cases. If there isn't already a deadline approaching, help her set one for this decision. The best artist is the one who knows when it is time to stop painting and move on.

- *The gossip.* DANGER, DANGER, DANGER! The best way to deal with this manager is to let her know you will not participate in gossip. You and she both have work to do. I found having a list of work-related topics to discuss will get her back on track.

Another way to speak your manager's language is to be current with the acronyms and terms applying to your department, the company, and the industry. I've worked in Marketing and Advertising, Manufacturing, Healthcare, Retail Sales, and Warehousing and Distribution. Each of those industries and their subsets have specific terms different from other places. Some companies even have a unique tribal language. Learning those words and their meanings (as I mentioned earlier) is another way to connect with your boss.

Chapter Summary/Key Takeaways

Before we can influence and develop a strong working relationship with our manager, we must open the lines of communication with her. If our preferred methods of communicating do not mesh with hers, we are doomed to being misunderstood, unheard, and discounted. It is worth the effort we make to adapt our style to get us listened to, understood, heard, and valued. We will also be better able to interpret our manager's meaning and intent.

In the next chapter, we will talk about ways to make our manager's job more productive and improve our team's environment at the same time!

Chapter 12: How to Pitch In!

"The way to achieve your own success is to be willing to help somebody else get it first."–Iyanta Vanzant

Managing Work vs. Doing the Work

You can help your manager by helping her get out of her own way. This is especially true if your manager was promoted from within the team.

Your manager may be much more comfortable getting down in the trenches than directing traffic.

One manager had a 'tell' whenever she was overstressed. She went back into the department and started working on the floor. She really thought she was helping out her team, but it backfired on her. The team quickly started to resent her intrusion and started to feel she was not happy with their work product. She even changed some tasks back to the way she did them when she was in the position. The newer process was much better, but the employees didn't feel comfortable telling the boss she was doing it wrong. They let her work off her stress episodes until the end of shift, then re-worked and fixed her mess the next morning.

What tasks are holding your manager back from focusing on directing, training, planning, reviewing, and completing all the paperwork and reports only she can and should be doing?

Here's where knowing the talents of the team is another tool in your toolbox. What routine tasks could others take off your manager's plate? Perhaps the reception desk could sort and collate the packets for the big meeting. Jane is a wizard at spreadsheets. Fred is the copier, shredder, and coffee-machine whisperer. George has a green thumb and just cringes when he walks by those sad plants on the manager's window. Jennifer is the fastest and most accurate data-entry person you've ever worked with.

Asking for help is not a weakness! Offering ideas to improve the productivity of the work unit helps spark creative thinking! She may not take your suggestion, but it just may start her thinking of other time- and energy-draining efforts.

She does not have to do it all. She actually has a whole team! By not using them to the best advantage, she is wasting resources and money. When she starts to rely on others, she is also showing she trusts and appreciates their talents. It is a fabulous way for your manager to build teamwork and a culture of helpfulness in the department.

After-Action Reviews (AAR)

This technique has been used in the military for years, and some of the best companies use this method after every campaign. It covers the three questions ANY review needs to answer (including performance reviews, but that is a different book).

- What worked well?

- What could we have done better?

- What did we need to do less of?

- AND add this one: What was a surprise?

Use this simple system to review events soon after they occur and when you have alone time. I like to write down my thoughts, and I find the historical review is valuable later, too.

Taking the time to reflect, dissect, and evaluate our actions and results is the way we learn. The more we know what works, what doesn't work, and what to look out for the next time, the better our next results will be.

If your company does not do this at regular intervals, suggest it. If your meetings drone on forever (yes, we've all been there!) then start by just answering those three things when it is your turn to speak. Others will catch on, and even the "long talker" will eventually be taken to task to just answer those questions, too!

Delta Plus

Delta Plus is similar to the AAR, with a slight difference I like. I first heard of it on the podcast "The Look and Sound of Leadership," by Tom Henschel. The question we answer in this method is:

What would our ideal result look like?

The trick here is this: the answer must be phrased as a positive wish! So instead of saying what you don't want any more of, the answer would be something like:

"I wish everyone would be five minutes early to meetings."

"I wish we could limit interruptions. Maybe leave our phones at the door?"

Meeting Preparation

I'm talking about the meetings where your manager will be in a room with her boss. Depending on your position, you may or may not be part of the group, but your input is valuable to your department's future either way.

Whether it is the weekly or monthly regular meeting or an important visit from the home office, this is the time when your manager WILL make an impression—good, bad or invisible! How can you help her advocate for your department and team? Here are some thoughts...

Find out what the meeting topic is. If you don't already know, ask. Your manager will note your interest, hopefully in a safe way and not as a threat to her job.

Ask how you can help prepare if a presentation is needed. Does she need handout copies made? Would she like to have someone video her practice speech? What data can you gather for her to present in numbers or percentages?

What are some positive changes you've noticed to drive future profit and cost figures? Numbers and percentages are the language of the C-Suite. Helping your manager have hard-number results and good estimated numbers based on trendlines will get her noticed by her superiors.

What are some pieces of information she needs to know from the others in the meeting? Having a list of pertinent questions will help the meeting be productive. Formulate some of the questions from the AAR and Delta Plus exercises above.

What Is Her Altitude? (What's Yours?)

Business strategy and planning sessions often use the word *altitude* when looking at the problem or issue from a distance. We are probably more familiar with these ways of describing altitude:

"Can't see the forest for the trees."

"She's down in the weeds."

"If it was a snake, it would have bitten him."

I recently heard a great description of what altitude means at work. It is the level of detail and the awareness of the environment around the work.

If we look at a map on the computer, we can zoom into the street level. This is where we can see outlines of buildings, names of businesses, and the fine details of a very small area of the map. In business, this is the level of the day-to-day job details. The person on the production line knows all the details and operating procedures for a specific job. Let's call this the 100ft level, where daily outputs are measured.

Now, as we zoom out on the map, we see the whole neighborhood; all the streets are there, but many of the details are no longer needed to understand the neighborhood. This is the level of the team leader or supervisor. They do not need to know all the details of each job, but they do need to know how those work together. Let's call this the 1,000ft level. Productivity measurements include more than just outputs at this level.

Zoom out a little more on the map, and we see the neighborhood is part of a small town. You can no longer see the individual streets, but the larger roads connecting the neighborhoods to each other are visible. This is the level of the next person in the hierarchy, the department manager. Let's call this the 10,000ft level. The manager needs to know how all the different teams work together in their department.

Zoom out even more, and we reach at least the 30,000ft level on the map. This is where the senior management needs to be, at a minimum. At this level on the map, most of our view is outside of town! We see other towns and the whole region around. If it is a weather map, we can also see those outside forces affecting us. The managers at this level coordinate and lead the departments as they work together to produce the company's products or services. But in addition to understanding the business, they can see the surrounding environment affecting the company in both the short and long term.

Back to the question:

At what altitude is your manager operating?

New managers often get stuck at the 100ft level, especially when they're promoted from within the ranks. They will major in the minor details while missing the larger implications of their decisions. Unless they can zoom out to better understand how their team fits into the larger map of the company, their ability to perform their management duties will suffer.

Although many supervisors and line managers can function adequately at the 1,000ft level, they are not considering or anticipating the needs of their manager. At only 1,000ft, she does not see the interconnectedness of the other sections or departments with hers in producing a quality product/service. Her decisions will not take into account those unintended consequences affecting others and rebounding negatively on her department.

A symptom of this is Silo Syndrome, where managers defend and protect their territory to the detriment of the department and whole location. Tom Formanek, CEO of Jenkins Auto Group, often reminds his 1,000ft managers,

"The enemy doesn't work for us. The enemy is across the street."

At 10,000ft, the department manager can see how all the areas work together to create a synergistic whole. She doesn't need to know how to do each job herself. She doesn't need to know all the details making the line or team function as a unit. Her job is removing the roadblocks getting in the way of her managers' performance and to coordinate and help the outputs of the various teams to meet her departmental goals for the business. Here is where her need to grow, mature, and expand her coaching skills becomes critical. Having a competent down line of leadership is necessary for her to operate at this level.

At 30,000ft, the senior manager is at the company's strategic development level. Here is where present meets future. Most of the map is outside of the town rather than in it. Decisions made at this level can affect the entire organization and have both short- and long-term implications. The most effective decisions at this level must also take into account the outside prevailing winds. I'm thinking here of emerging and/or disruptive competition, governmental interference, financial and other market trends.

Now, what about you? At what altitude are you operating?

It is just like traveling using a map. First: it is imperative to know where you are. If you're where you want to be, great. If not, you'll probably need to zoom out to where you want to be on the map.

I've noticed the better employees are operating at the right altitude *and* have an awareness of what zooming out to the next level looks like on their career maps. Being able to zoom out to our manager's level helps us see and understand her priorities and goals better. It also helps to see how our current responsibilities help drive those goals. The more we are aware of the higher-altitude thinking, the more interesting our day-to-day work life becomes.

We become more alert to happenings outside of the work place, too. A competitor's ad on TV or mentions on social media take on a new meaning to us personally. The news about a supplier or an upcoming change in the region causes us to contemplate the possible effects on our little piece of the map.

Chapter Summary/Key Takeaways

Our manager's success rests in our team's hands. If we help her, we are actually helping ourselves, our team, and the company as a whole. When we use the AAR and Delta Plus to dissect results, we can help plan for a better outcome the next time. When we pitch in to help our manager, she then has more time and mental bandwidth to increase her thinking altitude.

In the next chapter, we will discuss how to pick the right moment *and* how crucial timing is to the success of our efforts.

Chapter 13: When?

They say, "Timing is everything."

Yep, 'fraid so. I'll bet you even have an example in your mind right now. This is when all the work you have done to understand your boss's personality, strengths and weaknesses, needs, and values comes into play!

Once you start to 'read' your manager's non-verbal clues and understand her motivations, you can navigate your timing better.

Does your boss need her coffee before talking about anything?

Can you notice when she is so focused on work any interruption will be unappreciated?

Actually, these two things are minefields for anyone trying to discuss anything with me. I am usually pretty easygoing, but do NOT engage me then! It brings out the snarky, bad-tempered growl my husband knows so well. (I wonder why after so long he doesn't recognize these two danger zones?)

Ask yourself these two questions:

- When or in what situations does your boss react more positively?

- When or in what situations does your boss react more negatively?

Again, learning by observation as well as trial and error can really help you improve your influence with her. As you learn, the clues will become more obvious to you. Giving other team members a heads-up also helps you by expanding the number of influencers in your group.

Goal Setting

If you aren't familiar with the SMART goal-setting technique, just look for it online. SMART is an acronym for Specific, Measurable, Achievable, Realistic or Risky, Time-bound. This method of clearly defining your goals really does work. Of course, there are different tweaks and tips to using this method, but SMART works fine as far as it goes.

It does not answer the next part of the process, though—HOW? Just ask yourself this one question: **"What would need to be true that isn't true now?"** Boiled down to its most basic and essential, this question helps provide clarity any time we want to get from point A to point B.

117

I learned a valuable tool while working for a manufacturer. They decided to design a new product from scratch to complement their then-current line of products. (their Goal). Then they took a roll of butcher paper and mounted it along the longest wall in an unused area, transforming it into their bull-pen planning room. ALL departments (including customer service, accounting, building and maintenance, etc.) were given their own color of sticky notes to write each task they were going to be responsible for on a separate note. Then, using the sticky notes, they started at the END of the paper and placed the tasks needing completion by then. By using the question, "What has to be true then that's not true now?" they worked backwards. Thank goodness they used sticky notes! Some tasks had to done BEFORE the other tasks. Some tasks would take LONGER. Some tasks were removed. Others were added.

I left before the new product was completed but saw the rollout promotion a short time later AND within their timeline! Beautiful, functional, state-of-the-art.

Chapter Summary/Key Takeaways

Whether it is designing a new product or figuring out when to have an embarrassing conversation, it all comes down to timing. Once you have a goal with a "due by" date, working back from the future to now takes a HUGE and possibly SCARY goal down to easily manageable parts.

In the next chapter, we look at where to have the conversations, planning sessions, and other discussions necessary to move our goals forward.

Chapter 14: Where?

Answer: It depends.

The physical space where a conversation is held has a huge effect on the quality of the discussion. Is the location well thought out? Do you have the time blocked off? Is it a subject we can start out with first thing in the morning? Is it an emotionally charged topic requiring some down-time afterwards to digest and contemplate?

The Impromptu Blindside Meeting

One of the absolutely WORST places to hold ANY important conversation is an impromptu meeting in the hallway! No, no, no! Don't allow it. Suggested tactics:

- "This sounds really important. Let's meet at _x_ time in _x_ location."

- "I'm on my way to (bathroom, meeting, lunch, etc.). Send me a calendar invite for when we can meet."

- "You sound upset. Let's go to _x_ and talk privately."

- "I'm sorry—I can't discuss this right now."

By respecting the sensitivity of the topic, the privacy of the individual, and the other previous commitments you've already made for your time, you are displaying professionalism. As Tom Henschel would say, "The Look and Sound of Leadership."

Weekly One-on-One Meetings

This is of the best ways to standardize regular conversations with your manager at a certain time and location. A regular one-on-one meeting location is ideal and should be at the top of a manager's to-do list in order to connect with every team member on a weekly basis.

The manager's office or desk is the usual place. If you have something more personal, critical, or sensitive to discuss, then use a couple moments of the weekly meeting to suggest a short private meeting.

Meetings for Personal, Illegal, or Sensitive Concerns

Several views need to be considered for the location and timing. Some ideas are:

- Unused office

- Conference room

- Her manager's office – if serious or time-sensitive enough.

- Lunch room—off hours

- Before or after hours at the workplace

CAUTION: Think long and hard before deciding to meet your manager off premises. Unless people go out to lunch all the time and it is not unusual for the manager to sit with team members at a restaurant, do not do it. Someone will see, hear, or learn about the meeting. If your company hasn't squelched the gossip mill, this will be grist just too juicy for the busybodies to leave alone.

What if you haven't any pre-set time?

When do you need to 'nudge' your manager toward action or behavior? Again, it depends.

The HEADS-UP Conversation

Stop at her desk or give her a quick phone call. Is she oblivious to the chaos she just caused with her offhanded comment in the breakroom?

Those seemingly minor comments can cause major disruptions in the team's ability to focus on their work. Team members spend time conferring with each other to dissect the possible impact they infer from the statement.

CAUTION: The first contact needs to be verbal. Do not text, email, or leave a voicemail. Give her time to correct the situation quickly. If she hasn't taken steps within twenty-four hours, then it is time for an email or text with a reminder and your offer to help.

The Deadline-Approaching Conversation

Have this conversation in her office or other normal meeting location if her desk area is too noisy/busy/etc. Use an approaching deadline as a reason to schedule a sit-down with your manager. There are always deadlines, and once you have her attention, you may be able to discuss other performance issues at the same time.

Chapter Summary/Key Takeaways

Where the conversation is held says much about the gravity of the situation and seriousness of the subject. If a serious situation is discussed in a casual setting, it clues the other person it really isn't such a big deal. On the other hand, if someone makes a casual remark during a serious planning meeting, it gives those words extra weight.

In the next section, we will look at ways to move forward in our career-path journey.

PART V: Moving Forward

"If everyone is moving forward together, then success takes care of itself."–Henry Ford

Chapter 15: Change

"This too shall pass."

There's only one constant in our lives: *change*. Whether we are good at adapting to change or we resist it with all our heart, we can't stop change from happening. What's true today may not be true tomorrow. There are five stages of adapting to change:

- Averse—"No, no, no. Nuh-uh. I am never eating that!"

- Resistant—"Well, I'll eat it, but I'm not going to like it."

- Managing—"Looks like we're stuck with it. What do we do now?"

- Friendly—"Hey, this might actually be better. I can work with it."

- Seeking—"There has to be a better way. How can we change this?"

Since we cannot overcome change, we need to improve our ways to anticipate change, plan for change, adapt to change, and even enjoy and celebrate change. I think everyone finds change scary in some way, even when it is anticipated and looked forward to. So how do we learn to take the FEAR out of change coming into our lives?

For me, just looking back at what is true now that wasn't true before helps. Remember my big dilemma about my old car? I also look back on when a personal failure opened a fabulous opportunity for me. Just put some of your own examples in your mental toolbox. They are reminders you can pull out when needed. It certainly works for me.

Worrying about "what if..." just leads to anxiety and negative emotional reactions. Looking at the likelihood of the "what if..." and then making a contingency plan removes much of the fear and allows us to make more rational responses where a knee-jerk reaction would only make things worse.

Practice methods of taming your victim mentality when it automatically jumps to the worst-case scenario. What would be the BEST possible outcome? What can we do to help it become our new reality instead?

Much like the five stages of grief, everyone deals with change in their own way. By recognizing which stage of change acceptance we are in helps us move toward the next one. It is also true the "good old days" really weren't all that good. Change has brought us so many amazing things in our life. Look at changes through the lens of Friendly and Seeking stages.

Chapter Summary/Key Takeaways

Change is coming, and change is already here. How we adapt to change makes all the difference. We can use change to our advantage by improving our skills and helping others move toward change.

In the next chapter, we will discuss our need to be continuing to learn and grow as part of using change to our advantage.

Chapter 16: Learning More

This is the best time in the history of the world for access to amazing training and continuous learning opportunities! We all learn differently. And with the help of online audio, video, texts, and how-to instruction, we can avail ourselves of these resources in the formats working best for our learning style! I'm thinking of books, courses, local resources, coaching and mentoring, and even hands-on instruction. (Want to fix the lawn mower? There's a YouTube video for that!)

If you think about it, you already know which learning method you prefer. I'm primarily a reader but also enjoy video when it is a how-to demonstration. But my greatest stumbling block to learning something is needing to understand the *why*. Until I know why it is important or why it solves the problem, I just can't seem to wrap my head around the information. I won't be able to learn any process until I understand how it fits into the whole.

I talked with a young guy recently who told me he is totally a hands-on learner. In fact, he can't grasp any task until he does it himself. His manager at the new job had him read the instruction manual and watch a video but then was disappointed to find the new hire still couldn't do the work. When the young man finally admitted his learning style (he thought it was a disability and was embarrassed about it), the manager worked directly with him and walked him through the steps. He caught on at once and is now one of the top producers on the crew!

Negative Self-Talk

Why do so many people think they can't learn new things? Negative self-talk plays a part. "You can't teach an old dog new tricks," or "I'm not smart enough." But just because you had trouble catching on to a new idea or skill, it doesn't mean you can't learn. It is just a sign you weren't taught via your best learning method!

We learn new things all the time. What do you do now automatically or without effort you didn't know how to do before? How about your new phone?

Taking time to think about how you learn is so valuable! Rather than wasting time and beating our head against a wall, let's figure out how we best learn then use the best teaching tool we can find for all the new things we encounter.

Next question: **Do you know how your manager learns?**

Chapter Summary/Key Takeaways

Continuous learning is part of our lives, whether we think so or not. It is the tool helping us adapt to and embrace change in our lives. In fact, there is SO MUCH information out there, we best serve ourselves, our manager, and our stakeholders by focusing on the most critical needs.

In the next chapter, we will talk about how to determine where we will get a quick or big win, or the most bang for our buck. It is finding out what and where our strengths and weaknesses are.

Chapter 17: SWOT

(Strengths, Weaknesses, Opportunities, Threats)

Have you ever taken part in a SWOT analysis? It can be a great personal exercise and an interesting way to evaluate your manager.

My experience using this method has been during corporate strategic planning sessions. We have everyone in a room, often off site, and we brainstorm words and phrases falling into one or more of these four areas. I've used white boards and markers, sticky notes to a wall or poster, and even a scribe to write words the group shouts out.

The thing I've noticed in these exercises is what some people categorize as a Threat, others think belongs under Opportunities. Strengths can also be Weaknesses, depending on context and application.

In this exercise, you will understand yourself better and more clearly find places where your manager shines and where her blind spots are. It is your choice whether you perform this analysis on yourself first or on your manager. For simplicity, though, let's talk about your personal SWOT first.

Strengths and Weaknesses (Internal Attributes)

Can't think of the words to put down? Do a little research and reflection. Start with your strengths and weaknesses. These are your internal attributes. Hint: Look at the personality profile descriptions or the list of values back in Chapter 9!

Think of a time when you felt strong. What were you doing then? What words describe your actions and thoughts?

What about when you felt weak—not sickly, but powerless? What was the situation? What words and thoughts do you associate with the experience?

Threats and Opportunities (External)

These are those external actions and forces you have little, if any, control over. For example, interest rates are on the rise, the county is featured in a Best Places to Live magazine, or the region is in a drought.

Let's start with threats.

What and/or who in your life are stealing your time and sapping your bandwidth? If the situation continues, what could be the consequences?

What things do you worry about? Look back on Maslow's hierarchy of needs. Outside forces affecting your safety and security belong on this list. Relationship issues and things negatively affecting your reputation belong there, too.

Ok, now the flip side. Here's where you start to see opportunities to counter those threats on your list.

If you are worried about your value in the marketplace:

- Get certified

- Go back for the next set of initials to put after your name

- Join a professional group to network with others.

If you are over-stressed:

Decluttering your life could be such a liberating experience!

1. Simplify your environment. Donate, sell, or throw away anything you haven't worn, touched, or used in the last year. Scary? Here's what I continue to do periodically: Be ruthless in moving those items into piles, bins, or bags. Keep the containers in a corner for six months.

Then get rid of anything you have not pulled back out by then! I need the extra time to save myself from those regrets, and this takes the sting out of breaking up with my stuff.

2. Decrease those commitments no longer bringing joy. This alone increases your ability to pour your energy into new, rewarding endeavors. Again, start by just taking a break. Then after a few weeks, you can decide if you feel better without the commitment before pulling the trigger.

If you have financial stress:

If you are in a paycheck-to-paycheck situation, studies have shown this is the worst type of stress on your body and health! But there are things you can do to get out of this situation. One creative idea is to turn your hobby into a business. It may turn that cost center into a profit-making enterprise.

Next, get control of your finances with a spending plan (a.k.a. budget). You know the saying, "If you fail to plan, you are planning to fail." The best plan out there in my opinion is www.everydollar.com. Use the free, enter-it-yourself choice or their low-cost option to connect directly to your checking.

I recently found an old workbook from twenty years ago outlining my goals based on a similar exercise to SWOT. One of my top goals was to be able to travel to wonderful places. This was when we were living on my meager salary and in debt. In the intervening years, I can happily report, we were able to get out of debt and build a great retirement fund...and I have travelled to over thirty-six countries! It all started with that SWOT.

What Is Your Manager's SWOT?

The more clearly you know your manager, the more accurate your SWOT estimate for her will be, too.

Years ago, I had a senior manager who focused on and worried about her reputation. Getting something approved by her was one of the primary points of any successful presentation. It took me a while to understand proposed initiatives had to be good for her image for her to even consider approving them. Her reputation was her decision point. She even approved things not necessarily good for the business or the employees if she perceived her image was polished by them.

She craved the esteem of others to the extent she even risked her finances to appear successful in other eyes. She wanted to be one of 'The Joneses' others were keeping up with. She overextended herself and bet on a risky venture, thus causing her downfall. To this day, I wonder if I had just had a serious, candid SWOT conversation with her, would she have taken my advice?

When you know where your manager perceives her threats are, you begin to understand how it colors her view of her world. That knowledge is extremely valuable! Again, we all have our blind spots. Your manager has hers, too.

When you understand whether she gauges a situation as a threat or an opportunity, you can be the voice of reason to fill in a more complete picture.

When you understand how she views her strengths and where she feels her weaknesses are, you can more clearly plan your approach when discussing things affecting her negative self-talk.

Chapter Summary/Key Takeaways

A SWOT analysis helps us understand ourselves and our manager's motivations better. It also helps us plan for the inevitable changes coming at us and affecting our work and lives.

In the final chapter, we are going to take a hard look at the people in and affecting our lives.

Chapter 18: The Relationship Trap

If you're always busy taking care of others, how will you ever have the time to take care of yourself? There's a reason the safety reminder on the airplane tells us to put the oxygen mask on ourselves FIRST, before helping others on with their masks! When we are not at our best, we can't give our best efforts, wisdom, creativity, or even grace to others.

As we analyze our relationships with our manager and colleagues, we will often see other areas in our lives where the relationship is not best serving ourselves or the other person. So many times, the drama erupting in the workplace really isn't about anything at work. The stressors pushing the emotional reactions are based in our personal lives and relationships!

Time to Make a List

FIRST: Who and what are our stressors? How are they holding us back from being our best and wisest counsel for others at work? These can be workmates or your manager, but let's also focus on your relationships outside of work.

MARK: Which ones push our buttons? Which ones drain the life out of you? Which ones bore you? Which ones pull on your heartstrings until you ache?

EVALUATE: Which ones revitalize you and feed your soul? Which ones draw you down? Which relationships are moving forward? Which ones are stale and more of a habit? There is a dramatic difference between *empowering* the other person and *enabling* them.

All relationships move through different seasons as we grow and as circumstances change in our lives. If you have a fairly long list of relationships consuming your time and stealing your energy, it may be time to decide whether to invest more into improving the association or whether it is time to scale back the contact. The book *Necessary Endings,* by Dr. Henry Cloud, can help you examine these connections.

Of course, some connections need to be severed. Remember the statistic I referenced in the introduction? Around 75% to 80% of voluntary turnover is attributed to the relationship with the direct supervisor. Some people are just not ever going to get along well.

However, we all need to 'own' our contribution to any relationship, especially the one with our manager. We need to admit our livelihood is affected by and is proof we have a 'dog in the hunt' in developing a working relationship with our manager. By taking the time to develop at least some rapport with the manager, we can often accelerate our own as well as her career path by staying aboard with a good company and moving forward in our organization.

Chapter Summary/Key Takeaways

Interpersonal relationships push our emotional buttons to the point we can behave stupidly and out of control. We need to protect ourselves from being emotionally hijacked. Toxic relationships do not feed and nurture us. They steal our strength and energy away from us being our better selves. We have the power and responsibility to advocate for ourselves and our emotional sanity. When we just recognize how a relationship affects us, we can take the first step toward repairing, adjusting, or eventually severing those ties that bind.

My most stressful relationship was with my mother. Once I moved away from daily contact, we were more able to be friendly and cordial in our infrequent and brief interactions and phone conversations. I believe she would have agreed we got along great when we lived at least 1,000 miles away from each other.

Conclusion

The bottom line is: you can make an enormous difference in the workplace! All you have to do is open your eyes and ears to the possibilities.

Most of us like mysteries and detective stories. We're the hero in our own story, trying to figure out how to slay our dragons and save the day. What we often forget is that the other people around us are the hero in their own stories, too.

The question is what role are you playing in her story? As Donald Miller relates in his book *Building a StoryBrand: Clarify Your Message So Customers Will Listen*, the hero needs a trusted advisor, guide, or teacher to help point the way. There's Harry and Dumbledore, Katniss and Hamish, Luke and Yoda. If you think back on your life, you'll be able to name those very few people who positively influenced you, who helped you become the person you are today.

This is your role for your manager's story. She is the hero and you are the guide. It isn't rocket science, but it is a talent worth the time to practice and is so worth the effort to develop. I call it the Art of Managing Up.

Wishing you great health and relationships, financial stability, and peace,

Darlene

Epilogue

If all this is too much to think about at once, or all you really want to do is work where people play nice in the sandbox, remember things don't change unless things change.

I know you have a lot on your plate with all of the other things going on in your life. Let me suggest a baby-step approach.

If you haven't read Dale Carnegie's *How to Win Friends & Influence People* then TODAY get a copy! I prefer you buy one to keep and mark in, but the library certainly has one you can borrow for free. Used copies are inexpensive and available online wherever books are sold.

READ or re-read the book in segments of only one chapter each week.

Apply some of what we've discussed here to situations and conversations you encounter through the week.

Rinse and repeat.

Nothing stays the same, today is a brand-new game, it's time to change.

Bibliography

Carnegie, Dale. (Revised Edition 1981) *How to Win Friends & Influence People.* New York, NY. Simon & Schuster, Inc.

Covey, Stephen M.R. (2008). *The Speed of Trust.* New York, NY. Free Press Division of Simon & Schuster, Inc.

McChesney, Chris; Covey, Sean: Huling, Jim. (2012) *The 4 Disciplines of Execution.* New York, NY. Free Press Division of Simon & Schuster, Inc.

Van Edwards, Vanessa. (2017). *Captivate: The Science of Succeeding with People.* New York, NY. Penguin Random House, LLC.

Lencioni, Patrick. (2016). *The Ideal Team Player.* Hoboken, NJ. Jossey-Bass imprint of John Wiley & Sons, Inc.

Blanchard, Kenneth: Bowles, Sheldon M. (1993) *Raving Fans: A Revolutionary Approach to Customer Service.* New York, NY. William Morrow and Company, Inc.

Goleman, Daniel (2013) *Vital Lies, Simple Truths: the psychology of self-deception.* New Delhi, India. Bloomsbury India

Moore, Tony. (2018). *Culture in 4D: the blueprint for a culture of engagement, ownership and bottom-line performance.* Columbia, SC. Richter Publishing.

Tolle, Eckart (1999) *The Power of Now.* Novato, Ca. New World Library

Collins, Jim (2001) *Good to Great.* New York, NY. Harper Collins Publishing

Cloud, Dr. Henry (2011) *Necessary Endings.* New York, NY. Harper Collins Publishing

Definitions: http://www.businessdictionary.com
Miller, Donald. http://www.storybrand.com
Henschel, Tom. http://www.essentialcomm.com
Ramsey Solutions. https://www.everydollar.com
Lisa Thompson; www.lisathomsonlive.com
SCARF360: https://neuroleadership.com/research/tools/nli-scarf-assessment/
Taproot: http://www.taproot.com/archives/37771)
Gallup, Inc. www.gallup.com
State of the American Manager. (2015)
http://www.gallup.com/services/182216/state-american-manager-report.aspx

Acknowledgments

Special thanks to my draft readers, including: my sister, Jayda R. Messer; former co-workers and valued allies Jennifer Moore, PHR, and Suzanne Austin, CFO; and Tom Formanek, CEO and President of Jenkins Auto Group of companies. These readers took their valuable time to wade through my drafts, incomplete thoughts, and musings. They have pointed out my blind-spots, rabbit trails, and my many spelling and grammatical errors. Thank you all so much for your help.

An incredibly special thank you goes to my editor, Karin Nicely of Writing Nicely. She accepted this project although I was a first-time author with an ambitious deadline and a complete lack of knowledge of the publishing process. It was an education and a joy to read her edits and suggestions. Our conversations were a pleasure as she translated the thoughts into understandable prose. I look forward to working together again soon.

I want to acknowledge the influences of my many managers and bosses, many jobs, and companies I've worked with and for along my fifty-year span of working for a living. I've learned from all of them, both good and bad examples of managing techniques.

Three of my favorites are: Tom Formanek, CEO of Jenkins Auto Group, who worked with me in a true partnership while we built the supervisory team skills allowing for the company's quick expansion during the three years we worked together; Suzanne Dion Banks, CEO of Dion's Quik Marts, who showed me how a strong female can guide a company forward with style and grace; and a posthumous thanks to the late Larry Aiken of Aiken Management, who was the first one who showed me what true leadership looked like.

About the Author

DARLENE STUART GODDARD, SPHR, SHRM-SCP is the Regional Representative and HR Consultant for Employers Association Forum, Inc. (EAF). Darlene brings to her coaching over thirty years of HR managerial and executive experience in both manufacturing and non-manufacturing environments, including healthcare, retail, and distribution.

Darlene is a graduate of the University of Evansville with a degree in Communications. She's been a member of SHRM for over twenty years, achieving her SPHR credential in December 1996. She has maintained the SPHR designation through continuous learning and application of HR and sound business principles and received her SHRM-SCP credential in 2015.

She specializes in human resources consulting at all levels with proficiency in legal compliance, benefits, compensation, performance management, strategic planning, and organizational development, as well as recruiting, training, coaching, and mediation.

She serves on the Florida CareerSource Region 10 Board, where she is past Chair. She is an active member of Ocala HR Management Association (OHRMA) and has served on various non-profit and advisory boards throughout her career as part of her commitment to the communities and the HR profession.

Since 'retiring,' she has joined EAF as Regional Representative, continues to work as HR Consultant, coaching financial clients via the Dave Ramsey Preferred Coach program, and travels when her (still busy) schedule allows.

She lives with her husband, cats, and semi-tame wildlife in a rural community in Florida. Find her at: goddarddsHR@gmail.com, FB or LIn